Walter Warthog

Walter Warthog

BETTY LESLIE-MELVILLE

Doubleday

New York London Toronto Sydney Auckland

The publisher and the author wish to thank the following for
photographs appearing in this book:
Marion Gordon, pp. 32, 41, Franke Keating, pp. 12, 21, 45
and George Steele, p. 8
All other photographs are from the author's collection.

To place a credit card order of $25.00 or more, call, toll-
free, 1-800-223-6834, Ext. 9479. In New York, please call
1-212-492-9479. Or send your order, plus $2.00 for ship-
ping and handling, to the following address: Doubleday
Readers Service, Dept. FM, P.O. Box 5071, Des Plaines, IL
60017-5071. Prices and availability are subject to change
without notice. Please allow four to six weeks for delivery.

Published by Doubleday, a division of
Bantam Doubleday Dell Publishing Group, Inc.
666 Fifth Avenue, New York, New York 10103

Doubleday and the portrayal of an anchor with a dolphin
are trademarks of Doubleday, a division of
Bantam Doubleday Dell Publishing Group, Inc.

Library of Congress Cataloging-in-Publication Data
Leslie-Melville, Betty.
Walter Warthog/Betty Leslie-Melville.—1st ed.
p. cm. Includes index.
Summary: Describes how the author and her family
established a friendship with a warthog at their home
outside of Nairobi and how the relationship continued
for eight years, embracing the hog's offspring.
1. Warthog—Juvenile literature. 2. Leslie-Melville,
Betty—Juvenile literature. [1. Warthog.
2. Leslie-Melville, Betty.] I. Title.
QL737.U58L47 1989
599.73'4—dc19   88-34637   CIP AC
ISBN 0-385-26378-3
0-385-26379-1   (lib. bdg.)

To Liza, my granddaughter
who makes the sun shine so
brightly in my life
and who made the warthog so
happy too, by giving
him her toy giraffe

Introduction

I LIVE IN NAIROBI, KENYA. NAIROBI IS THE capital city of Kenya, a country on the east coast of Africa. My house in Nairobi is just like many houses in the States, except we have giraffe, warthogs and a leopard which live on our property.

I live in Africa because I love animals and I save endangered species. Endangered species are rare wild animals which are being killed in large numbers, such as the rhino for its horn and the elephant for its ivory tusks. They are about to disappear from the earth. Once there are no more elephant or giraffe or rhino, you can't create others, so it is necessary to save them now.

One particular endangered species we saved is the Rothschild giraffe. My house is called Giraffe Manor because some of these rare giraffe live on our property. They even put their heads in the second-floor bedroom window and over the lunch table. Tourists coming to Africa on safari stay at my house. It is the only place in the world where you can touch and feed wild giraffe.

One day while I was busy giving the giraffe a bottle of milk, a huge warthog appeared on the lawn and scratched himself on the wall. Warthogs are a kind of wild boar which live in Africa. They are related to pigs. Like pigs warthogs are very smart, but unlike pigs they can be very dangerous.

I became very good friends with this fully grown wild warthog. I don't know of anyone else who has had a warthog friend. This book tells how it happened.

Walter scratching himself.

Chapter One

THE DAY AFTER I HAD FIRST SEEN THE huge warthog on the lawn, I walked out the front door of the house we had recently moved into in Nairobi, and standing very close to me was the same enormous warthog. He had eight-inch tusks and must have weighed two-hundred pounds. I was very frightened. Warthogs are fierce fighters. I knew that one had just killed a donkey across the valley from us, and that a few months before, another had killed a man. They use their tusks for digging and fighting, and protruding from their lower mouth are two huge razor-sharp teeth called scimitar tusks with which they fight and slice.

Trembling, I ran back into the house and looked out the window at the beast. He was kneeling down on his two front legs, as warthogs always do to eat, nibbling our grass, which is mostly what warthogs eat. When he had had enough food, the warthog ran off, with his tail sticking straight up in the air like a mast. I told my husband, Jock, and my children about him. The next day he was back, and the next day,

Walter thinks our grass is delicious.

and the day after that. We always watched him out the window, and although he looked mean, he seemed very nice.

Every day for two weeks he was on our lawn, coming closer and closer to the house to eat the succulent grass by the front door, but every evening at sunset he would run, with his tail straight up in the air, through the woods adjoining our property to his house in the woods where he slept. Warthogs live in big deep holes dug by ant bears, or as they are also called, "aardvarks." Warthogs back down into these holes to hide there and sleep all night. It is very dangerous to walk by a warthog's hole because if he is in it, he will feel trapped and zoom out charging you.

Finally my husband and children and I got up enough courage to go out our front door when Walter was near and carefully creep by him. He ignored us. Gradually we became nonchalant about coming and going with the warthog just a few feet away. We would always say a cheery "Hello," and he would just look at us. He never tried to charge.

Walter Cronkite, a famous newscaster, and his family came to visit us. When Walter saw this enormous warthog grazing by the front door, he spent a long time watching him. He was so intrigued we decided to name the warthog Walter after him. From then on, when the warthog was

Walter thinks our grass is delicious.   *Franke Keating*

nearby, we would always say a cheery "Hello, Walter."

Soon, when Walter Warthog was on the lawn just a little ways away from us, we began putting some grain, which we fed our horses, down on the grass. When he saw us doing so, he'd come running, with his tail straight up in the air, and gobble it up. He loved it!

One day after Walter had been there a few months, I got up a lot of courage and held the grain in my hand. Seeing it, he began to walk toward me very slowly. I was so scared that my hand was shaking so hard I could barely hold the grain. Would Walter charge me? Would he even try to kill me? He came right up to me, then very gently he put his head down and politely took the food from my hand. I was thrilled. Every day after that I fed Walter like this. Then after a few weeks of feeding him from my hand, I got up a lot of courage again and gently stroked Walter's nose. It felt like sandpaper, but he seemed to like it. However, he never wanted me to go behind him—he wanted to keep an eye on me. So I always stayed in front of him.

Walter and I became very good friends.

■ ■ ■

Chapter Two

WALTER CONTINUED TO COME TO OUR lawn every day, wandering around, getting to know the dogs and cats, horses and the giraffe which also lived on our property. Since we have no fences, two of the endangered Rothschild giraffe we had saved, named Daisy and Marlon, wandered about freely. They were very curious about Walter. When he first arrived, they just watched him from a distance. Then one day when he was on our lawn eating the grain which they also love to eat, they sauntered up to him. Since Rothschild giraffe are eighteen feet tall, they had to spread their legs very wide apart to lower their long necks down to have a close look at him. Walter was afraid Daisy and Marlon were going to eat his food, which was what they had in mind. He snorted viciously and thrust his great tusks at them. They were afraid, and quickly jumped up and walked away. After that they knew he was boss, and Daisy and Marlon never tried to eat his grain again. Mostly, giraffe and warthogs eat different things—giraffe eat leaves of trees instead of grass. So one day when there was no grain on the lawn and Walter was eating the grass, they tried to make friends again. This time, when they lowered their heads next to him, he didn't snort or scare them. This time he just looked at them. And soon they became friends too.

Our son named our two kittens Maisy and Darlin. Every time we'd call them, the giraffe would come, or when we'd call Daisy and Marlon, the cats would come. The giraffe and cats were friends and would eat out of the same bowl, until Walter came along. He would walk up to the bowl, snort and thrust his tusks at

Hello, Walter!

them, scaring all of them away, then eat all their food himself. He was very greedy. So we put their bowls high up in a tree the cats could climb and the giraffe could reach, but Walter could not get to. He would just hang around at their feeding time, looking pathetic and hoping we'd give him some of their grain too, which of course we did.

When there wasn't any food around, Walter never showed anger toward the cats or the giraffe or the horses. In fact, he liked their company and would sit on the lawn in the sun with all of them. They would all drink from the fish pond together.

Shirley Brown was an exception. Shirley Brown was our black Labrador. She didn't like the giraffe or the cats or the horses, and she hated Walter Warthog. She was jealous because we were paying so much attention to him instead of her. She was very glad she was the only one allowed in the house, and when Walter arrived on the property, she wouldn't go outside at all. We had to gently drag her outside on a leash and fuss over her, all the while ignoring Walter. Soon she began to go outside by herself again. But she would run back into the house if Walter even started to walk in her direction. However, she would sit in the sun on the lawn with the giraffe and the cats and the horses. Finally, she would join the rest of the animals even when Walter

Walter arrives at feeding time.

was there, but she never sat close to him. In time, she and Walter became friends sort of, but not very good friends.

Our horses liked the giraffe and the cats and Shirley Brown, but they were afraid of Walter at first. When they'd roll on the lawn, Walter would watch them with interest, but what interested him most, of course, was their food. He seemed to be able to tell time and always appeared at the proper place at the proper feeding time for each different animal. Every evening at the horses' feeding time, Walter would be there.

One of our horses, named Quicksilver, was unaccountably getting thinner and thinner, even though he was eating like a horse. The vets found nothing wrong with him. We wondered, what weird disease did he have? Finally we discovered the trouble. As Walter watched the horses being fed every evening in their stables, he observed that Quicksilver had an odd habit—he would eat his food only from a bowl on the ground, instead of from a bowl placed up on a shelf. So Walter had dug himself a tunnel into the rear of Quicksilver's stable. He would watch for horse-feeding time with beady eyes, then rush around and enter the stable through his secret tunnel while the other horses were being fed. Like everyone else, Quicksilver also knew Walter was boss. So once inside, Walter would act ferocious, back the terrified Quicksilver up against the far wall and guzzle the delicious meal.

We put cement around Quicksilver's stable so Walter couldn't get in anymore. Then Walter began sneaking into the tack room where we kept the grain in large burlap bags and pulling the bags over so the grain was on the floor. Then he would devour it. When Walter wasn't looking, we moved the big burlap sacks of grain from the tack room to a toolshed and tied them up. But within ten minutes he had detected the hiding place, opened the door, pulled the burlap bags down onto the ground, ripped them open with his tusks again and was gorging himself. At dusk that evening, when he went off with his tail straight up in the air, we moved the food bags

Walter guzzles Quicksilver's food.

to a shed far from the stable where Walter had never been. But the next morning, about five minutes after he arrived, we found Walter guzzling the food in there too.

He was growing very fat.

Finally, we had to buy huge metal drums for the grain and locks for the doors, and make the food shed a maximum-security area. From then on, Walter received only one big meal of grain every morning, plus whatever he could beg throughout the day. He would sit outside the front door waiting for us. Sometimes he would get up and scratch himself on the little stone wall. Sometimes he would sit on it and wait for us to appear. If he heard us leave by the back door, he'd run around to intercept us, look up at us endearingly and nudge us gently on the thigh to remind us we hadn't given him enough to eat.

It is said the smartest animals are apes, followed by porpoises, and next pigs. Warthogs, being in the pig family, are very smart—certainly smarter than dogs. And Walter was a genius. Of course he knew his name. If he were out of sight when we wanted to see him, we'd call and he'd come running. He was always delighted to see us. He loved us to scratch him and talk baby talk to him.

This lovely relationship went on for about two years. "But he's so ugly," all our visitors would say. We didn't agree, we thought he was beautiful—because we loved him. And all those who came to know him soon thought Walter Warthog was beautiful, too.

Mmmm, good!

Chapter Three

THEN ONE DAY WE DIDN'T SEE WALTER at all. We didn't see him the next day, nor the next day, nor the next. We called and called him, but he didn't come. We began to worry that he had been poached. Poached means killed by people who shoot animals with poisoned spears or guns, or catch animals in snares. Snares are thick heavy wires which are made into a loop, then tied to a tree in the woods. When a warthog or another animal runs by, its head gets caught in this loop, which pulls tight around its neck. Then the animal is trapped there. When the poacher who set the snare checks and sees he has caught something, he kills it. Warthogs are good to eat; they taste like roast pork. The poachers are often poor people who don't have enough money to buy food, so they catch animals to eat. Poachers also want to sell warthogs' ivory tusks, which are used to make handles for expensive bottle openers.

Daisy and Marlon's mother and father, and many of their relatives, had been poached. Since the two baby giraffe didn't have anyone to take care of them, we were raising them. When great numbers of one type of animal are poached, there are soon only a few left. These are called an endangered species. One day Daisy, who was already an endangered species, caught her ankle in a snare in our woods. Luckily we found her and were able to cut the awful snare off before the poachers found her. They would have killed Daisy and eaten her, and with the hair from her tail they would have made a bracelet to sell.

We knew there were people who would think

Daisy's foot in a terrible snare.

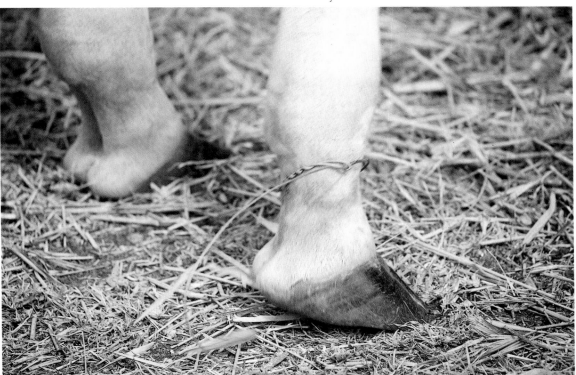

Walter would make a delicious meal and that his big tusks would bring them a lot of money.

Also, the leopard which lives on our property loves to eat warthogs and dogs. We had been told he had already eaten quite a few warthogs in the area and the dog next door. But leopards sleep in the daytime and hunt at night, so Walter and Shirley Brown never went out at night. So naturally, between the poachers and the leopard, when Walter disappeared, we were very worried about him.

For four days we searched and searched the forest, and called and called him. We couldn't find him anywhere. Then on the fifth day, as I was about to search the woods again, Walter came walking very slowly and sorrowfully onto the property. His tail was not up in the air. I cried out to him, "Walter Warthog, where have you been?"

As he got closer, I saw that around his snout was a ghastly snare. The dreadful steel wire was cutting deeply into the bleeding flesh behind his great white tusks and was locking his jaws completely shut. It had taken him four days to snap the heavy wire free from the tree to which it was anchored. It was a good thing the poacher hadn't gone back yet to see if he had caught anything in his terrible snare. Walter was in much pain. Since he had not been able to eat or drink for all that time, he was also weak and thin, a shadow of his portly self.

"Oh, Walter! Poor Walter!" I ran toward him and stroked his injured face. He looked so sad. I ran into the house and got a pair of wire clippers. Walter just stood there, this great wild wounded beast, holding up his nose to let me try to cut through the snare, but I wasn't strong enough to do so.

I called Jock at his office, and our vet. Both came immediately to help. The vet began to prepare his blow-dart gun to tranquilize Walter, so Walter would become unconscious and we could remove the snare. Walter just stood quietly beside me making pathetic little whimpers.

Looking around at the thick forest surrounding us, Jock gestured despondently. "But," he said to the vet, "when the dart hits, he'll be frightened and run flat out to his hole in the woods. We don't know which hole he lives in, and he can run faster than we can. If you can't give him the antidote medicine in five minutes, he'll die. Let me just hold him and try to get the snare off."

"No," answered the vet. "That is a wounded wild beast, perfectly capable of killing you."

"Walter wouldn't hurt us," we both told the vet. But he didn't believe us and kept on preparing his blow-dart gun.

"Don't tranquilize him," I begged.

"The alternative of letting him starve to death is worse," said the vet.

I began to cry. "I don't want Walter to die."

Jock put his arm around me and said to the vet, "I'm going to try getting it off myself. If I fail, it's your turn."

He ran to the house and got a hammer. I held a bowl of grain high up for Walter. Of course he couldn't open his mouth to eat, but it made him lift his head up to try. Jock was then able to hook the claw end of the hammer into the snare under Walter's chin.

Walter jerked backward violently, pulling Jock flat on his stomach on the ground, but Jock still held on to the hammer. Walter dragged Jock across the lawn! Just as Jock was unable to hold on any longer and was about to let go of the hammer, the snare came loose, but it still remained around Walter's snout. Walter wheeled around and headed straight for Jock at full speed.

"Look out!" we cried. "Walter's charging you! Get up!" But before Jock could get up, Walter had reached him. Then suddenly Walter stopped, leaned down and with his head gave Jock a gentle nudge on his arm—as if to say thank you.

The vet was very surprised. We weren't. We knew Walter wouldn't hurt us.

The vet sprayed purple medicine in his wounds, and Jock and I fed him lots of water and food.

Walter got food and comfort from everyone after his dreadful experience.

We patted his face and scratched his back and comforted him with baby talk. He was so happy. Every day he was back again with us.

Six more months passed, and again Walter didn't come in one day. The next day he walked in with another snare around his snout and looked at us endearingly. This time my sons just sat on his back and pulled the snare off. Walter looked at them lovingly and gave them a thank-you nudge. He was so sweet. I couldn't believe that a long time ago I used not to like warthogs. But Walter Warthog had captured my heart. I thought he was beautiful, both inside and out.

Chapter Four

AFTER WALTER HAD BEEN WITH US ABOUT three years, he arrived one morning with a mother warthog and three babies . . . Walter's family. We were very surprised, because scientists had told us mother warthogs and their children often live in one group and that the males usually live alone. But Walter stayed with his family and brought them around to us for some grain and attention. He was very considerate. The babies were just a few weeks old. They were adorable, hairy little balls zinging around in short bursts of frantic energy like overwound toys, with their tails straight up in the air. None of the babies would come near us. They ran every time we

Mother and two of her three babies.

approached, but they ate all the grain we put on the lawn for them, with great enthusiasm.

A few months later, I noticed Walter and his entire family digging away furiously just outside the sun room where Jock and I were eating lunch. Wildlife specialists had told us how smart warthogs are, but they had neglected to tell us that warthogs are also excellent water diviners and engineers. The water from our bathtub drains underground and is never seen again. However, Walter detected subsurface moisture, and he and his family began their excavation. They were not looking for drinking water, since the fish pond, from which they quaffed gallons, was only twenty paces away. They wanted a mud wallow. As they dug, water began to seep into their hole. When it was big enough, they got in it and sloshed and twisted in the muddy water. Sometimes they just lay in it on their backs with their feet sticking up in the air. Surprisingly pigs are very clean and have no odor at all, but on bath days, Walter and his family smelled like Gardenia Bath Oil, which I always used in my bath.

Walter and the mother and three babies were a very happy family. They stayed on our lawn eating, sleeping and playing together all day every day for about a month. Then one day only two little babies arrived, all alone. Later on we found the third baby and the mother dead in the forest in snares. Would the mother's remaining babies survive without her? It was so sad watching the two little things scurrying about the lawn, then kneeling down on their two front legs trying to nibble grass—since they had no mother's milk to look forward to. We felt so helpless, what were we to do?

We needn't have worried about them because Walter adopted them. He took excellent care of them, which is extremely unusual for a male

What a wonderful time in the mud wallow!

warthog. But then, Walter was very unusual. He would romp with his babies on the lawn, and when they flopped exhausted, he would clean them with his teeth. If he lay down to snooze, the babies would clamber all over his great fat lolling body before curling up next to him to sleep. He was a very good mother. Every evening all three would run off together, with their tails straight up in the air, and hide in their ant bear hole for the night.

Jock and I had two friends who were nuns, Sister Helen and Sister Marie. They were in Nairobi helping the poor people and teaching African schoolchildren. Often they would bring some African children who lived in the city and had never seen a wild animal to see the giraffe and the warthogs. One day when they were visiting us, Sister Helen said as she was watching the two little orphan warthogs eating the grass, "They must be good Catholics—see how they

Two little orphans all alone.

Running off to the ant bear hole to sleep.

kneel to say grace?" So we named the motherless little babies Helen and Marie. But as they gradually came closer and closer to us, we discovered they were boys. And soon Helen and Marie, the two little warthogs, were eating from our hand and became our friends too.

Walter must have told all the other warthogs in the area that our property was a good safe place for them, where they could also get a lot of delicious free grain, because one day another family arrived—mother, father and three tiny babies. We put food down on the lawn for them and enjoyed watching the babies play with Walter's sons, Helen and Marie. The little ones all chased each other around the lawn, running around in circles, all with their tails straight up in the air. But if we'd go near any member of the new family, he'd run off.

One day when the new family arrived, one of the youngsters' legs was dangling, twisted and bent. It was obviously broken. He was holding it up, pathetically trying to run to keep up with his mother and father and two sisters, but soon he would become exhausted and need to lie down. Although we knew how to get warthogs out of snares, we didn't know what to do about a broken leg. We called the Game Department, and Operation Warthog began on our front lawn. Have you ever tried to catch a young warthog with a protective mother nearby? It was extremely difficult and dangerous for Sam Ngethe of the Game Department, but finally, with a long string used as a lasso he caught the poor little thing by the foot. It took several people to seize him. Then we popped him into a large Macy's box, tied it with rope and drove him to our vet.

Bored with the endless procession of cats and dogs he usually treated, the vet was delighted to

Caught at last!

see a warthog again. But soon he was wishing it were a cat or a dog. What a battle! The fierce little thing kicked, bit, struggled, butted and nearly escaped three times. Four people had to hold him down in order to get an anesthetic needle into him, and still he resisted. Jock and I put on lead-lined aprons and helped hold him for the X rays which the vet needed to decide what had to be done. After studying the X rays the vet had purple medicine and a cast on the poor thing's leg in no time. "A broken foreleg on a warthog is very nasty," he told us. "You'll have to keep him indoors for six weeks."

Indoors? We thanked him anyway. When we asked for the bill, he said, "The game belongs to all of us—there'll be no charge." I thought that was very nice, but I noticed he didn't offer to keep the little warthog in *his* living room.

Jock did not want our house to be used as the convalescent home. Instead he decided on a building near the stables with a cement floor, which we covered in wood shavings and sand. A table was in one corner, and we put a cardboard box sideways under it so that the young warthog could have a small house to hide in, something of great importance to animals in captivity. We served the angry little warthog delicious grain and milk laced with bone meal and vitamin drops. In return for our kind attentions and good food, he charged us furiously, as nimbly as if he had no cast, butting our legs, biting at our hands and behaving like a miniature torpedo run amok.

The next morning we found him sitting *on* the table, looking mean. We wondered how on earth he had climbed onto it, but we didn't have to wait long to find out. As I took food in to him, he bounded off the table and charged me, bruising my shins badly as he collided with me. He had his mind set on escape. So he took off across the room and tried to scale the wall like a gecko. Even with his cast on, he got five feet up the wall before falling back on the cement floor. We were astonished but worried about his hurting himself. But if we put him in a stall with a dirt floor, he would have burrowed out in no time. So we brought in more sand and shavings and barricaded the window too, something we would never have dreamed a warthog could do until we saw his spider-man act.

The following morning I peeked through the window at our fierce piglet. To be honest, I was nervous about going in, but he was lying peacefully in his box, his little stomach bulging with breakfast, and his cast *off*. So it was back to the vet again, another hassle, another cast, and six more weeks of trying to escape. Understandably he never became friendly. We had taken him from his family, put something awful on his leg and kept him alone in a little room. He hated us.

Finally the vet took his cast off, pronounced his leg healed and said that he was ready to be released. We took him home in the Macy's box, put it sideways on the front lawn, opened it and sang "Born Free" as he ran off into the woods. He never came back to us again. He didn't want anything to do with us. But from time to time we saw him in the woods, and we knew we had given him what was now a happy warthog life.

The little warthog left his purple cast behind.

Chapter Five

LIFE WENT ON UNEVENTFULLY IN OUR warthog world for another few years, except that greedy Walter, trying to get some spilled grain which had fallen between the metal rungs of the foot scraper of our front door, caught his tusk in it and couldn't get it off. He walked around nonchalantly, with his sons Helen and Marie, for a few hours wearing the doormat scraper like a hat in the wrong place before we could get him to stay still long enough for us to twist it off.

Next to be in trouble was Marie, who was now almost three years old. Walter brought him up to the house, with his nose in a snare. "Well," said Jock, "the hazards of being a warthog certainly are high." Marie, who was in pain,

Sam Ngethe prepares the antidote.

would not let us near him to try to get the snare off. This time we had to let Sam Ngethe fill his blow-dart gun with tranquilizing medicine. He aimed it at Marie and whizzzz . . . zingggg . . . ping—it got him! Marie ran, with the dart right behind his head and his tail straight up in the air, screeching like a, well yes, a stuck pig. He staggered and stumbled in a flurry of legs and trailing wire, until he reached the edge of the fish pond. There he teetered for twenty seconds, so sleepy his tail began to droop, and then he flopped unconscious into the water. Jock, the children and I ran to the pond. Walter and Helen, Shirley Brown and the horses ran with us. We all watched as Marie was hauled out before he drowned. We cut the snare off, put some purple medicine on his cuts and gave him the antidote. He came to and charged us. We ran in different directions and got away from him. Walter certainly hadn't taught him very good manners.

Then Shirley Brown disappeared. We were afraid she had been taken by the leopard or caught in a snare in the woods. We searched the forest all day, and called and called her—all to no avail. We were very upset. Finally at dusk I said to Jock, "Shirley Brown doesn't go off in the woods by herself or outside at night, and I don't think the leopard would come right up to the house in the daylight, so maybe she isn't in the woods after all. Maybe she's been bitten by a snake or is sick or something and is around here." I crawled on my stomach under a huge bush not too far from the house, and sure enough, I saw what I thought were Shirley Brown's eyes glowing at me. "Shirley Brown's here!" I called,

Marie, unconscious, is hauled out of the fishpond.

and with that I heard a loud, ferocious warthog's savage roar, "Arummmph . . ." It was not Shirley Brown at all but a fierce warthog—charging me. I realized I had unwittingly found a warthog's hole. But it was impossible for me to get out quickly from under the thick low bush. So I crouched and turned, figuring I would rather be slashed up by its knifelike teeth in my back than in my front. Trembling, I waited for the terrible attack. Nothing happened. The vicious warthog had come for me but then veered. Shaking, I crawled out from under the bush, and there stood *Walter.* He was shaking too. When he had got close enough to pick up my scent, he realized it was me and swerved out the other side of the bush. We both stood there quaking, and then we nuzzled each other. Later on that evening our son brought Shirley Brown back; he had taken her with him for a picnic.

The next morning Walter was in the living room. He was standing there, happily looking over the place to see if he wanted to move inside with us. We loved Walter, but we just couldn't have a wild boar in the house. So we quickly put some food outside, and Walter got the idea he would not be fed inside. Since eating was his favorite thing, he didn't come in again.

A few months after that, I heard a knock at the door, and when I opened it, there wasn't a person standing there at all—it was Walter! Yet again in another snare. This time he just came to the house and banged on the front door with his snout, asking for help. He knew we would get it off, and we did.

Eight years had passed since Walter joined our family and gave us so much joy. Then one day he didn't come to us, nor did he come the next, nor the next. We called and called, and searched and searched the woods, but we never found him. We never saw Walter again. We learned he was poached. His great tusks are now a bottle opener.

We cried and cried. We miss him so much.

Helen and Marie growing up.

But his sons, Helen and Marie, have grown big. They are five years old now. Marie has not been very friendly since his bad experience of getting in a snare and falling in the fish pond. But Helen is. He is outside our front door every morning waiting for us. He scratches himself on the wall, then sometimes just sits on it and waits for us. He comes when called, and not only eats from our hand but loves us to touch and scratch him and talk baby talk to him, just like Walter. He looks just like Walter too, so we changed his name to Walter Jr.

We love him too.

And the other day, Walter Warthog, Jr., was in our living room.

Conclusion

BECAUSE OF OUR LOVE FOR WALTER AND the giraffe, and our great interest in saving endangered species, we formed the African Fund for Endangered Wildlife. Many people in America help us save the endangered species. Having saved the Rothschild giraffe, we are now trying to save the elephant and the black rhino, the most endangered animals in Africa today. In 1977 there were 22,000 rhino in Kenya and today there are fewer than 500. As we did with the giraffe, we are now moving the rhino to the safety of game parks. We put them in huge areas surrounded by electric fences, and we have to keep guards on them twenty-four hours a day so they won't get poached.

The elephant is being poached terribly now. They are being poached for their ivory. If people didn't buy bracelets or ornaments made from ivory, the elephants wouldn't be poached. So please do not buy anything made of ivory.

We decided the best way to stop all the poaching is to educate the children. We got this idea when we had some workers refinishing the floors in our house one day. I heard one of them, a woman, screaming outside. I feared a warthog had butted her or a giraffe had kicked her, and I ran toward the door just as she came running inside. She was trembling and very frightened. "The biggest dog I have ever seen is following me," she gasped. It was Daisy, our giraffe. But how would she have known what a giraffe is? Most Africans don't have enough money for a car, and no one can enter a game park unless they are in one, and even if they get a ride with someone else, they don't have the $3.00 entrance fee. They can't afford television, even children's books, and there are no zoos, so how would they know what a giraffe or a warthog or an elephant is? Eighty-five percent of the Africans never see the wildlife. So that's why we decided the most important way to save the animals is to educate the people.

We built the first educational nature center in independent Africa, and each month we have two thousand African school children out, free, to see and feed the giraffe and the warthogs, and to learn about conservation. We tell them how thousands of visitors from all over the world come to Africa on safari to see the animals, and that if they have all been poached and there are

Daisy loves it when the children come to the educational center.

Franke Keating

none left, visitors won't come to Kenya. And if there are no safariers, the people won't get jobs. Tourism is a huge industry that provides the Africans with jobs. They are game rangers and wardens, and they also drive for the tourists in game parks, wait tables in the lodges, build roads to the lodges, grow food for the visitors in the lodges and do many more jobs.

After the schoolchildren have fed the giraffe

and warthogs, we show them films on conservation, and then they are taken on a walk through our forest with a teacher. Some of the children are so poor they have never been out of the city and have never seen even a tree, much less an animal. Not only are they thrilled, they have learned why they should not poach the animals.

Wouldn't it be terrible if all warthogs were killed to become bottle-opener handles? And wouldn't it be terrible if *all* the animals were poached and our grandchildren would have to ask, "What was a giraffe? What was a warthog?"

But with the help of people who care, perhaps we *can* save the animals. It costs a lot of money to buy electric fences and pay rangers to guard the animals, but even a dollar helps.

If you would like to help, send your tax-deductible contribution to:

> The African Fund for Endangered Wildlife
> 1512 Bolton St.
> Baltimore, Maryland 21217

If you would like to come on safari, write to us for additional information. You can stay at Giraffe Manor, as my house is now called, and the proceeds from your stay will go to help save endangered species.

Daisy, who has babies of her own now, will put her head in your second-floor bedroom window and thank you, and Walter Warthog, Jr., will give you a gentle little thank-you nudge, too.

The whole happy family at Giraffe Manor.

Betty Leslie-Melville has lived in Africa for twenty-seven years and has lectured and written about East Africa and Ethiopia for the last seventeen years. With her late husband Jock, she founded the African Fund for Endangered Wildlife (AFEW), which has already saved the Rothschild giraffe and is currently trying to protect the highly endangered black rhino and African elephant. They established the first educational nature center in independent Africa, which is host to 2,500 African schoolchildren each month. In 1983, Betty was honored by Protection of Animals Worldwide (PAWS) as the Outstanding Person in the Realm of Conservation.

Betty has also been a cameraman, associate producer and consultant for documentary films and television specials. Her own life has been the subject of a television special. She has written seven books, five with her late husband. *Daisy Rothschild,* her first book for children, tells of her extraordinary experiences as the first person to successfully raise wild giraffe. She has three children, and with her youngest son runs a safari company that organizes photographic safaris to East Africa. Her home in Nairobi, now called Giraffe Manor, is the only place in the world you can touch and feed a giraffe. It is open to safari-goers who are willing to make a donation to AFEW.

■ ■ ■